詩 瓣
Poem Petals

王 祥 麟 著
馮 馮/英譯

Siam Lim Heng (Canada)

English Translation by Peter Faun(USA)

文史哲出版社印行

The Liberal Arts Press

國家圖書館出版品預行編目資料

詩瓣 = Poem Petals / 王祥麟 (Siam Lim Heng)
著；馮馮（Peter Faun）英譯. -- 初版. --
臺北市：文史哲, 民 95
　頁： 公分. --（文史哲詩叢；74）
中英對照
ISBN 957-549-680-9(平裝)
ISBN 978-957-549-680-7(平裝)

885.351　　　　　　　　　　　　95011869

詩 瓣 = Poem Petals

著　　者：王祥麟（Siam Lim Heng）
英譯者：馮　馮（Peter Faun）
出版者：文　史　哲　出　版　社
　　　　http://www.lapen.com.tw
登記證字號：行政院新聞局版臺業字五三三七號
發 行 人：彭　　　正　　　雄
發 行 所：文　史　哲　出　版　社
印 刷 者：文　史　哲　出　版　社
　　　　臺北市羅斯福路一段七十二巷四號
　　　　郵政劃撥帳號：一六一八○一七五
　　　　電話886-2-23511028・傳真886-2-23965656

實價新臺幣一六○元
中華民國九十五年（2006）十二月初版

一位自修天才藍領詩人

王祥麟是一位來自新加坡的加拿大人，是在溫哥華的藍領工作者，從事勞工維生。他只有初中教育背景，在工餘時間喜歡上圖書館及逛書店，廣泛地閱讀，主要興趣是宗教、哲學與文學。

他起先拿給我看他自修寫作的幾頁詩句向我請教，我很坦白告訴他，寫的不怎麼樣好，只是塗鴉。我推薦他研讀古今中外的名詩，特別是推薦他讀日本古代的芭蕉和尚的詩，與印度泰戈爾。

後來祥麟多次來呈閱他的新作中文詩篇，我很訝異發現這個塗鴉作者已經變成真正的詩人。他的詩句很簡潔，有哲學味，甚至有些開悟禪味。佩服之餘，我就主動要為他的詩譯成英文，讓更多讀者欣賞與了解。

現在已經是越來越多刊物與報章刊登他的詩作。他已經成為小小詩句的先驅，引發不少後繼者。我曾經在大學擔任過講授英詩教授，但是我必須坦承並非一個詩人。在翻譯祥麟的詩句，我已盡力而為，當然距完美很遠，不過我希望，最少足以幫助非中文讀者了解他的詩。他可能仍未成為一個偉大的詩人，但是他是值得賞讀的。本詩集唯一缺乏的是浪漫的詩句，他很少寫。

馮 馮（PETER FAUN）

夏威夷

Title of the book: Poem Petals
Author: Siam Lim Heng (Canada)
English translation: Peter Faun (USA)

Introduction

The author Mr. Siam Lim Heng is a Canadian talented self-taught blue collar poet originated from Singapore. As a blue collar worker in Vancouver, with only secondary school education, he spends his free time to browse libraries and book stores and does extensive reading. His major interest is religion, philosophy and literature.

He came to show me a few pages of his self -taught writing of poems and asked me for comments. I told him frankly that they were only scribbling. I advised him to study ancient and modern Chinese poems and international poetry too if he wanted to become a poet. I recommended the poems by Bosho, the ancient Japanese poet-monk and Tagore of India.

Siam Lim Heng came back to show me batches after batches of his new poems written in Chinese. I was amazed to find that the scribbler has become a real poet. His poems are concise, philosophy , and with touch of zen, and enlightenment. I was so impressed that I offered to translate them into English to let more readers enjoy and understand them. More and more publications and newspapers have now accepted published his works, and he has become a fore runner of mini-poems to inspire other poets.

I used to be a professor of poetry at university, but I must admit that I am by no means a poet. I have done my best to translate Siam's works but far from perfect. I hope, at least good enough to help non-Chinese readers to understand his works. He may not be a great poet yet, but worth of reading. But what is missing in this collection is romantic poems which he seldom writes.

Peter Faun.
Hawaii

王祥麟著《詩辮》馮馮/英譯

Siam Lim Heng《Poem Petals》

English Translation by Peter Faun

目　　次

CONTENTS

第一輯：孤獨園

Volume I：Garden Of Loners

孤獨園

一片葉子
繫一個念頭

寧謐，悄然落在
兩片葉子之間

Garden Of Loners

A leaflet
With an idea.

In serenity, falls quietly down
Between two leaves.

生　命

狂風搖樹
浪拍岩石

潛伏的意識
是否觸及那脈動的活力

Life

Crazy storm rocks trees
Waves whip cliffs
The hidden consciousness
Does it touch
The pulsation of life?

吶　喊

月
冷凝如石
緩緩吐出

濤聲

Shouting

The moon
Frozen as a rock
Slowly utters

The sounds of waves.

本　質

陽光下的影子
是黑夜

Essence

The shadow under the sunlight
That is the dark night.

活潑潑

雀躍的浪花
沿著沙灘
將足印的沉重

揹走

Vigor

Jubilant waves
Lick away
The heavy load of footprints
Along the sandy beach.

浮 雲

慵眠
如石頭燙熱的體溫

夢，在大地
敞開

Floating Fleecy Clouds

Indolent and drowsy
With the body-temperature as scorching stone

Its dream spread
Over the Great Earth.

風　鈴

能不釋懷麼？
諷嘲
揶揄

釀出淙淙清泉

Wind Chimes

Can't you feel relieved?
That sarcasm
And teasing

Ferment gurgling and clear spring stream.

湖　泊

沉默地
收藏風雨

Ponds

Quietly
Collecting storm and rain.

秋

禿枝
化作千爪
誓將擄走葉子的風

撕下

Autumn

Bald tree branches

Turned into thousands of claws,

Vows to tear down

The wind that captured the leaves.

夜

皓月當空下，一場即興揮毫的潑墨雲海騰空而起。

Night

Under the bright moon in the sky,
An improvised ink-splash painting of cloud rises.

熱　情

冰冷的風
冰冷的浪
向冰冷的峭壁
投于千億瓣冰冷
激昂的浪花

Passion

Icy cold wind
Icy cold waves
Towards icy cold cliffs,
Bombarding millions of pieces
Of icy cold wave petals.

失　憶

夢來過
沒人記得

Amnesia

Dreams have visited,
But no one remembers.

太陽神

彈轉地球于指尖
逗出人間

日升
日落

The God Of Sun

Twisting the Earth in its fingers tips
He retreats from Earthling

Sun rises
Sun sets.

火　柴

寸木，怎能遏阻
眥裂嘶響的怒火？

煙
蛇立作答

Matches

How can tidbits of wood deter explosion, of
Wide-opened eyes and roaring fire of anger?

To answer,
The smoke rises to do cobra dance.

二　拍

其一：輕

誰
一顧腳下
聆聽
小草的真言

其二：惘

誰
醉入狂風
踏著
凌亂的拍子

Two Beats

First: Take it lightly

Who

Looks under

To listen to

The honest words of little grass.

Second: Lost in the thoughts

Who

Drunken and staggering in storm

Doing

Broken steps.

時　光

自水龍頭的隙縫悄悄躡步
跨出
一個踏空的日子

滴答作響

Time

Sneaking thru a faucet's crevice
Astride
An empty day

Tick-tag and tick-tag.

夢

一根不經意的羽毛
跌落在
虛空的睡姿

旋舞

Dreams

A piece of unmindful feather

Falls in

Vague sleeping posture

To do waltzing.

秋　霧

不及反應霧的擁抱
失措的黃葉
無　　風
自　　落

Autumn Fog

Unprepared for embrace of fog,

Yellow leafs helplessly

Even there is no slight breeze.

扎 記

夢遊------若有所思的腳步

跋扈------行走的仙人掌

鱷------呆若浮木的兇徒

自言自語------浮出水面的思想

Footnotes

Sleep Walking------Paces with thoughts in mind.

Bossy------Walking cactus.

Crocodile------The villain with appearance of a floating log.

Soliloquizing------Thought surfacing the water.

失　眠

每一瓣浪花
是腦海翻騰的聲念

每一個妄想
是心房塗鴉的寄情

無盡的夜
無休的掙扎

Insomnia

Every petals of wave
Are roaring in mind.

Every false thoughts
Are the graffiti.

Endless night
And endless struggling.

抱　枕

渡過
夢的巨河

卻遲遲不肯鬆開
懷裡的漂木

Pillow Clenching

Across
The wide river of dreams

Yet reluctant to let go
The drifting wood in the arms.

風　鈴 II

隱形的心靈捕手
在五味雜陳的意識裡
拎起

一支歌

Wind Chimes II

Invisible catcher of mind

Rings a song

In the consciousness of feelings.

掃　帚

曾經，幻想是
一匹奔馳騰躍的駿馬

而今，清閒地
陪著枯葉邊走邊聊

Broom

Once with the fantasia
As a galloping fine horse.

Now leisurely
Accompanies the withered leafs.

西　瓜

殷紅
不是熱血

是一座冰山
在體內分崩離析

Water Melon

Freshly red
But no warm blooded

Like an iceberg,
Disintegrates within.

第二輯：雨絲

Volume II：Drizzling Poems

☆

地面的水灘向路過的白雲說：「我是風雨打造的鏡子。」

Puddle to the bypassing white cloud: "We are mirrors
made by storms."

☆

挽不住的夕陽，跌落眷戀的嘆息。

怦然的滿天星斗，如潮動的鼓舞。

Unsalvageable sinking sun, with falling sighs of
attachment.

With all the sudden appearance of clusters of stars,
exciting as tides.

☆

玫瑰示人以嬌艷，刺針卻透露了牠心底的恐懼。

A rose demonstrates its dazzling beauty,

But its pricks disclose its fear deep at heart.

☆

一葉彎彎笑笑的青草，

是陽光牽引你探出洞隙之外？

抑是生命的動力，把你推出在天地之間。

Green grass with bending smiley leaves,

Is it the sunlight attracts you to come out of the crevice?

Or, is it the motivation power of life,

That pushes you between the sky and the great Earth?

☆

白晝借出空間于黑夜，

黑夜歸還了它。

The day lends out its space to the night,

And the night returns it.

☆

貪慾是佔據森林的霧，不曾有一片葉子屬于它。

Greed is the mist occupying the forests,

But none of the leaves belongs to it.

☆

「雨，您劈里叭啦說些甚麼？」

「與大地別後重逢的話。」

"Hey! Rain, what are you splattering yakking about?"

"Only a chat with the Great Earth upon reunion."

☆

啣著信仰的麻雀；遠離陸地，

飛向遼闊的海洋，

忖想那是唯一神聖的國度。

The sparrow carrying faith in its beaks, flying away from
land,

To the vast and holy oceans,

In search of the sole kingdom of God.

窩在悄無動靜的葉尖底下，

是悶悶不樂的風兒麼？

Nesting beneath quiet and motionless leafs

Is that the bloomy wind?

☆

一面光滑的大理石是失去理解力的鏡子.

A smooth shining marble is just a mirror without understanding power.

☆

情慾視蚊子的吮吸為親蜜。

Desire considers mosquito's sucking as intimacy.

☆

靜止的空氣，隱藏狂勁的意志。

伺時迸激，割山拔木；萬鈞的力量。

Stillness of air hidden violent will.

Awaiting opportunity to spurt to lacerate mountains,

And eradicate woods with thousands tons of power.

☆

岩石感覺流動的風，

風感覺不動的岩石。

Rocks feel the flowing wind,

The wind feels the immobility of rocks.

☆

一日之後，雲再度燃燒。

一年之後，楓再度燃燒。

唯獨青春的火焰；

不復再度燃燒。

After one day, the cloud will burn again,

After one year, the maple will burn again

But the flame of youth

Never rekindle.

☆

葉面稱帝的螞蟻，霸氣縱橫三吋。

An ant as a king of a leaf, stretching its power three inches across.

☆

神殿巍然矗立在虹的殘柱。

Temple stands still on the ruined pillar of rainbow.

☆

桀傲之海豈作一杯茶水忖度，

狂嘯之風焉是一穴死寂等閒。

舉澎湃如山岳之嘯浪；

搖撼沉沉心魂。

The proud ocean never gives consideration to a cup.

The howling wind is not a cavern of dead silence.

The mountain-like tidal waves;

Shaking the depth of any hearts and souls.

☆

流水的目標不在于大海-------在不斷的流動過程。

The aim of the flowing stream is not the ocean,

But the continuous process of flowing.

☆

生命的氣息，在凜冽寒冬中孤挺的枝椏撲翅。

The breath of life is flapping its wings on the twigs in the

cold winter.

☆

古老的問題：

「我是誰？」

古老的答案：

「業力。」

An ancient question:

"Who am I?"

An ancient answer:

"The power of Karma is me."

☆

「蟬，甚麼令你長鳴？」

"Oh Cicada, what makes you buzz all day?"

☆

新婚燕爾的螳螂太太，

幸福滿足地愛撫飽脹的肚皮。

Mrs. Mantis, on wedding day,

Heartily satisfied caressing her filled belly.

☆

渴望的杯，期待的酒；

散盡香醇於空中無盡未來的時光。

Glass of thirst, wine of expectation,

Releasing all flavors in the air and endless future.

☆

烈日下曝曬的仙人掌，湖底止息的龜鼇。

可知；麻木難以消除疾苦，止水亦非生命真諦。

The cactus exposed to scorching sun,

The sunken turtles holding its breath in water.

But, numbness can never eliminate sufferance,

Still water is not the truth of life.

☆

渾身刺針的仙人掌；蜂群奉若神明。

Thorny prickly cactus, Worshipped by wasps as deities.

☆

也只有那風狂，才催得動百媚千嬌的櫻瓣，一一化作雪花飛舞。

Only the crazy wind can blow the beautiful cherry blossoms to fly and dance like snow flakes.

☆

月的凝視；引動奔騰不絕的潮來潮往。

The gaze of the moon pulls the incessant tides up and down.

第三輯：摩訶止觀

Volume III：Maha-Chih Kuan

摩訶止觀

月波，蕩
入眸中

Maha-Chih Kuan (Great Perceptivity)

Moonlight on ripples,
Floating into eye-sight.

無　明

執蛛絲力可隔海
著一塵足以遮日
　　火花
抖餘多少落索的灰燼
在無盡的焦土

Ignorance

With one piece of spider's web to separate oceans

With a speck of dust to cover the sun.

Sparks,

Shaking off ashes of loneliness,

On endless scorched lands.

千　手

月光
深深
敲擊，
緊閉的
窗扉

Thousand Hands

Moonlight
Deeply
Knocking,
On tightly closed
Window。

鑿

刻　　乃過去的記憶
痕　　是意識的溝槽
延　　續一個自我
伸　　延一道業力

Sculpturing

Carving　　-- the memories of the past

Marking　　-- the ditches of consciousness

Extension　-- of an ego

Stretching　-- a power of Karma.

法　性

江河
奔流在

夢裏
夢外

Dharma Nature

Rivers
Running

In dreams and
Outside dreams.

湖

雨
點點刺激
盪開
　　圈圈悒鬱
　　陣陣焦慮
滴滴荅荅，兀自煩燥
柳樹輕輕點化：
　　　　無非一體

Lake

Rain

Drops by drops

Expanding

Circles of melancholy

Ripples of anxiety

Tic-tac, and tic-tac, what worries

Light touch of the willow tips :

        Nothing but the same entity.

眼 前

誰
在觀察中
搬起文字
築一座座妄想

誰
在注視中
多般言語
說一套套妄念

誰
在觀察中
不攜文字
直入實體本質

誰
在注視中
不作一語
圓融一切法相

The Present

Who
In observation
Piling up lettering
To construct castle of illusion.

Who
In gazing
Using various languages
To preach all sets of delusion

Who
In observation
Ignoring lettering
And penetrating the substantial truth.

Who
In gazing
Speaking no words
But covers all forms of Dharma.

舞 池

思潮變幻的燈光
迷惑詭譎的煙幕
節奏強勁的妄想
狂跳不停的雜念

Dancing Floor

Changing fantastically is the lights of thoughts' tides.

Treacherous and bewitching are the smokes,

Strong beats of rhythms of delusion,

Non-stop dancing of earthy ideas.

閉　　關

心　停止語言
　　收起文字

所在
足下方圓一呎

所修
鼻樑上方一吋

Seclusion

The heart
Languages cessation
Letters retrieved

Whereabouts
One square foot under the feet

Cultivation?
One inch above nose ridge.

窮開心

如果
妄想是空性

如果
妄念是覺悟

我是一億萬個佛

Pleasantry

If
Illusion were voidness,

If
Delusion were awakening,

Then I would be ten billions of Buddha.

當　下

涅槃
不是未來

淨土
掛在眼睫毛端

The Instant

Nirvana
Is not the future

Pure land
Is hanging right on one's eye-lashes.

苦集滅道

幻影，
禁錮在水面。

Duhkha, Samudaya, Nirodha and Marga
(Spiritual shackles)

Reflection of mirage,
Imprisoned on water surface.

方　外

松樹托腮沉思
白雲外傳來
風的笑聲

Out of the Earth

Pine tree is brooding, holding its chin,
Here comes the laughter of the wind
From distant white clouds.

寂

瀑布的暴跳聲，
一吼入林。

Serenity

The thundering of waterfall,
Shouting into forests.

水尊者

跡近瘋狂的行徑
囫吞擲石
嘴角浮笑

The Respectable One in Water

Behaving nearly like crazy

It swallows thrown stones

With slight smile at its mouth.

十 方

一滴雨；
一個落腳的地方。

Ten Directions

One drop of rain,
A landing place.

第四輯：俳句

Volume IV：Haiku

倒　影

山，
在顫抖。

Reflection

Mountain,
Is shivering.

下 雪

雪花，沉
入空海

Snowing

Snow-flakes,
Sinking into the ocean of voidness.

仲　夏

皺波無語，
蜻蜓拍過蘆葦。

Mid-Summer

Creased ripples are wordless,
A dragonfly flips over reeds.

流 星

一劍，
割破夜幕。

Shooting star

One blade of sword,
Slashing open the curtain of the night.

獨木橋

直樹，
橫躺。

A log bridge

A piece of straight tree trunk,
Lying across.

星　星

洪荒凝聚，
光亮過去迴置未來。

Twinkling Stars

Congregation before time begins,
Shine in the past, the present and the future.

諦　聽

月光，
躡入大地的夢囈。

Listening

Moonlight,
Entering the dream murmur of the Great Earth.

陰 霾

黑潮壓海，
白雨吞山。

Haze

Dark tide overcastting the sea,
White rains devouring mountains.

夕　海

火霞映海，
白浪平沙。

Evening Sea

Fiery afterglow is shining on the sea,

White waves are washing smooth sandy beach.

溫哥華的俳季

春：

春櫻如雲，
低低浮在街上。

夏：

獨唱的剪草機，
引發大合唱。

秋：

秋裝大清銷，
一葉不留。

冬：

山麓一夜白髮，
頓成話題。

Haiku Season of Vancouver

Spring Time:

Profusion of cheery-blossoms
Floating like clouds lowly on streets.

Summer Time:

Soloing lawn-mowers
Trigger big-chorus

Autumn Time:

All autumn fashions are for dumping sales
Leaving not one single piece of leaf

Wintertime:

Mountains turn white-hair over night
To become subjects of gossips.

秋

寒冽的北風漸漸收緊
楓葉的宿命
如火蔓延

Autumn

The cold north wind is tightening up

The maple leaves' destiny

To turn a fiery spread.

街　燈

光禿的小島
在夜的大海中
守著潮退

Street Lights

The bald safety-island
Awaits ebb-tide
In the ocean of the night.

雪 人

堆雪的孩童
以他們的形像
造人

Snow Man

Children playing in snow
Are making a man
In their own images.

情巳逝

在這晴朗明媚的週末
昨日狂歡的愛情
像空了的汽水罐

Love faded

In this bright and nice week-end,
Ecstasy of love yesterday
An empty can of pops.

傳

溪澗
冷冷流動
雪融的冰囑

To Pass On

The brooks blowing coolly
With thawing ice jam.

冰淇淋

大人與小孩
在魔術棒點化下
紛紛變成狗

Ice-Cream

Grown-ups and kids
Under the spell of the magic wand,
Turn into dogs.

檢　閱

模仿雁群的戰機
一字斜飛
人字排

Air inspection

Fighter-jets imitating wild geese
Form V-shaped formation
Flying side-way.

搖籃曲

水波柔柔
在靜穆的沙上
拍著輕韻

Lullaby

Soft ripples of rhythm,
Caressing gently
On serene sands

凋瓣的怨恨
彷彿已不置可否
花開的芳醇

Separation

Hatred of withered petals
Seemingly unconcerned
About blooming fragrance.

雪中行

一張張小嘴
尾隨貓的身後
七嘴八舌

Walking In Snow

So many small mouths
Are following the cat
To deliver chatters.

雪 後

枝上的白雪
佯裝春天的櫻花
逗出知更鳥

After The Snow

The white snow on tree branches,
Pretending to be cherry blossoms of spring time
To tease robins.

日　曆

每天換不同的面具
說是
新面孔

Calendar

Changing different masks everyday
To declare that
They are new faces

床

不設防的監獄
軟禁了三份之一
人生

Bed

The prison without fense

To incarceration

One-third of a life time.

棉　被

夜夜溫存
是否等於披上
一層親密關係？

Cotton Comforter

Warm keeping every night,
Is it wearing
A layer of intimacy?

鼾

瘋狂轟炸每一寸夜
勢必奪回
白日裡的失地

Snoring

Crazily bombard every inch of the night,
To regain
All territories lost in daytime.

愛情一旦腐朽

愛情一旦腐朽
百種蜜釀
儘化淚罈

One Day When Love Decays

One day when love decays
All honey nectars
Will turn into tears

窺 孔

伸出長長的觸角
探測
門外的陰晴

Keyhole Peeping

Stretching long tentacle to survey
The shine or overcast outside.

畫中月

陽光照耀著
近于透明的面孔
陌生而熟悉

Moon In Daytime

Sun shines on
Nearly transparent face,
So strange yet so familiar.

晨

打開窗扉
像鬱金香敞開花瓣
吮吸陽光

Morning

It opens the window
To absorb the sunshine ray
like tulips blooming.

睡　貓

蜷如鵝卵石
沉臥在
夢的流域

Dozing cat

Curled up like a pebble
Soundly reposing
In the realm of dreams.

融

燭焰，在
夜的呵護下
光華倍增

Combination

Candle flame
Under the protection of the night
Doubling its brightness.

芽

戟骨林立的魚化石
經春天的妙手
重生細鱗

Sprouts

Spiky bones of fish fossils
By warm touch of the hands of springtime
Regrow small scales.

無　垢

寒夜裡
纖彎的新月
一弧明亮

Immaculacy

In the chilly night
Slender crescent new moon
A curve of brightness